# DREAM MAKERS

## YOUNG PEOPLE SHARE THEIR HOPES AND ASPIRATIONS

SELECTED AND ILLUSTRATED BY
NEIL WALDMAN

BOYDS MILLS PRESS

For Kath, whose sensitivity, intelligence, and intuition
were invaluable in sifting through
the many remarkable entries
— *N. W.*

Published by Boyds Mills Press, Inc.
A Highlights Company
815 Church Street
Honesdale, Pennsylvania 18431
Printed in China


Publisher Cataloging-in-Publication Data (U.S.)

Waldman, Neil.
    Dream makers : young people share their hopes and aspirations / selected and
illustrated by Neil Waldman.—1st ed.
[32] p. : col. ill. ; cm.
Summary: To celebrate the one hundred fiftieth anniversary of The Children's Aid Society,
children express their dreams in prose and poetry.
ISBN 1-59078-178-3
1. Children's dreams, Poetry—Juvenile literature. 2. Children's writings, American.
3. Children's poetry, American. (1. Dreams, Poetry. 2. American poetry, Collections.)
I. The Children's Aid Society. II. Title.
811.54 21   PS591.S3.W146   2003
2003101074

First edition, 2003
The text of this book is set in 16-point Baskerville Cyrillic Upright.
The illustrations are done in watercolor on Arches cold-pressed watercolor paper.

Visit our Web site at www.boydsmillspress.com

10 9 8 7 6 5 4 3 2 1

## PREFACE

For the past one hundred fifty years, The Children's Aid Society has been helping children to realize their dreams. Working with 120,000 New York City youngsters and their families, Children's Aid provides a wide range of programs and services, striving to offer each child the opportunity to become a happy, healthy, and successful adult.

The idea for this volume grew out of a meeting I attended with friends from The Children's Aid Society and Boyds Mills Press. As I focused on my dream for this book, I asked young students in New York City and around the country to express their dreams in prose and poetry. Many hundreds of submissions were received, from the South Bronx and Harlem to the Deep South and the Rocky Mountains.

Although only forty-two pieces of writing could be included in this volume, The Children's Aid Society has graciously agreed to post all the entries on its Web site, www.childrensaidsociety.org/dreammakers. A list of the schools that participated in the project appears on the last page of this book.

*—N. W.*

A dream is something you want to happen

A dream is something creative and

something you can't ignore

A dream is the future

A dream is an astonishing miracle

A dream is something to wish for

A dream is your secret thought

A dream is your mind and memory

A dream gives you confidence

A dream awakens you every day

A dream is what keeps you alive

*Amanda Esquilin,*
*fourth grade*

It is my dream that in fifteen years I will
be a cowboy. I will ride horses and give one to
my grandfather.

*Adrian Rivera,*
*fifth grade*

If you let go of dreams

everything you dream about

will go away

forever

Without dreams

life just wouldn't be the same

People just wouldn't be themselves

So hold tight to dreams

because you might go far

*Melissa Tierney,*
*fourth grade*

My dream is to have a lifetime supply of

chocolate.

*Emma Thacker,*
*fifth grade*

I'm waiting by the telephone
hoping for an important call.
The TV is on, but everyone is quiet.
It is 11:15 at night.
We're all tired, but we're staying awake.
I say to my mom,
"We've been sitting here for over two hours.
I wonder if they'll ever call?"
Suddenly, the phone rings. It rings again.
We all stare at each other.

I pick up the phone.
"Hello?" I say.
"Hello," a man says.
"I'm calling to offer you our congratulations.
You're the first pick
of the New York Yankees."

I hang up the phone and start to cry.
My dad stares at me with a worried look.
"Oh no," he says. "Bad news?"
"No," I smile.
"I'm going to play for the Yankees!"

*Matt Stovall,*
*fourth grade*

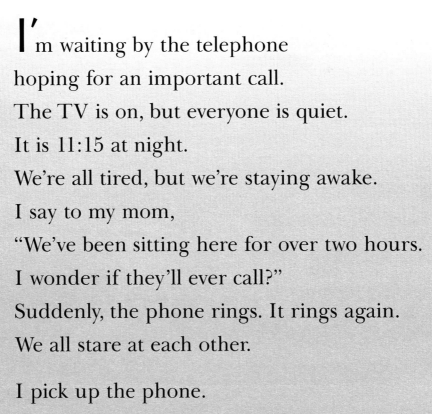

A dream, a fantasy
floats in my head
Turning over and over
in my mind
I fly through the air
with the wind in
my hair
I sing a short song
as I fly along
Flying through the air
in my dreams

*Ava Bynum,*
*fifth grade*


I dream that someday I will make a car that
can fly.

*Christopher Diaz,*
*third grade*

My deepest dream is to make the world a better place for children and grown-ups.

Tommy Rich,
third grade

Is not the true spirit of a Dream Maker to look at life, the world in which we live, and work for a better community, nation, and world?

Josh Garza,
sixth grade

I dream of world peace. I want everybody to get along and live peacefully together. I think this could happen if people tried their best to listen to each other.

Carl Ceraolo,
fifth grade

"Lucy Chong, please come up to the stage," the announcer's voice booms from the loudspeakers. I waltz up, tears streaming down my face. I have discovered the cure for cancer, and I am about to receive the Nobel Prize in medicine.

Suddenly, I am back in my bedroom and I think, *That's where I want to be in fourteen years. But how will I get there? I'll have to do a good job in school. Then I'll get a scholarship. I'll go to college and become a chemist. Finally, I'll find the cure for cancer. It will be hard, but fun. I'll donate most of the million-dollar prize to find cures for other diseases. It will be a blissful life, finding the cure, seeing people helped, seeing them happy.*

Then I think, *Better finish my homework if I want to find the cure.*

*Lucy Chong,*
*sixth grade*

I have a dream

The forests are large
Trees are no longer needed for paper
All species thrive
Man lives with the animals
The animals live with man

The world is at peace
War is a thing of the past
Soldiers return home

There is no selfishness
Money does not go to those who horde
but to those who need
The earth is shared
No land is owned
There are no more jails
Greed is no longer
Neither is hatred

Just one lesson is taught in schools:
How to care and be kind
to others and the earth around us

*Matt Ritter,*
*fourth grade*

My perfect world
My place of dreams
will have a monkey driving
my limousines

In my mansion
there will be a pool
with a shooting fountain
so blue and cool

Outside my mansion
is my own private town
where I am king
and wear a crown

When crickets chirp
and the sun goes down
fireworks sparkle
in my perfect town

*Zach High,*
*seventh grade*

When I was young in the Bronx, chocolate chip cookies had more chocolate chunks than they have today. I can still taste the chocolate melting in my mouth.

When I was young in the Bronx, my friends and I would have double Dutch tournaments that would last for hours on hot summer afternoons. I remember how my ponytails would slap me in the face as I jumped to the rhythm of the ropes. The bottoms of my feet would pound the pavement until they were numb.

When I am older I will create new memories by making my dreams come true, but I will still recall the chocolate chip cookies and double Dutch contests of the days when I was young in the Bronx.

*Zoe Adams,*
*sixth grade*

# Hello

My name is Mr. Jurdon Lemar Hill
I am a multibillionaire

I'm married with children and have a house
in every city
My children get a pair of the newest sneakers
every week
We will never be poor again

In my main house there are five floors
and each floor has two big rooms

My dog has its own maid
and its own one-story house

I own many companies
even the cable company
and out of the kindness of my heart
I give everyone in my neighborhood free cable

Right now my life is in its prime
and I love it!

*Jurdon L. Hill,*
*eighth grade*

When I grow up I'll be an art teacher because
I can help people show how they're feeling,
just by drawing on paper.

*Dominique Edouarzin,*
*fourth grade*

I wish my dream was a picture waiting to
be painted.

*Sherry Gurule,*
*fifth grade*

It is 2015
I am a singer
I sing romantic songs
My voice is like a bird
Singing in the air

*Ismmaelly Guaba,*
*third grade*

Last night I dreamed of the days when I was young in Jamaica. The tropical rain was cool on my hot skin, refreshing and peaceful. The rain gave us a chance to calm down and rest from our game of hide-and-seek.

We took shelter from the misty rain under leafy mango trees and ate juicy mangos as we waited for the sun to shine again. Sometimes we would run down the road to Auntie's house to listen to stories about the moon and the stars.

But now I awaken from my dream. I am in my apartment in the Bronx. I rub my eyes, far from the rolling green hills and clean fresh air of Jamaica. I miss the colorful little "doctor" birds singing joyful songs. I miss helping Grandma crack coconuts on the rocky garden wall by the veranda.

Dreams of when I was young in Jamaica always fill me with joy and sadness.

*Annesha Lee,*
*sixth grade*

Now my only dream is that someday my children will grow up with no violence in their heads.

*Reyna Henriquez,*
*eighth grade*

Deciding which dreams to follow can be one of the hardest decisions in life.

*Laura Becker,*
*fifth grade*

Remember that dreams can come true!

*Stephen Beutel,*
*fifth grade*

In ten or fifteen years I see myself as a rap star, to help my family and just rap for fun.

*Richard Ramirez,*
*fourth grade*

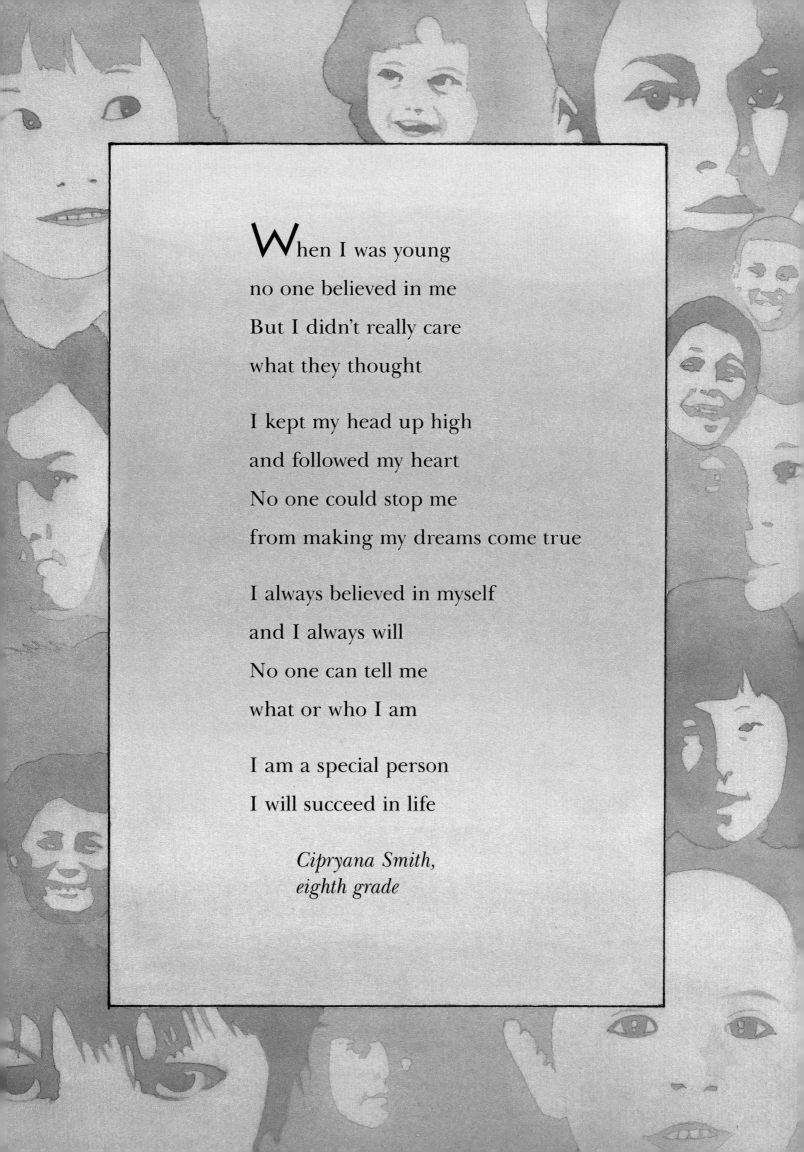

When I was young

no one believed in me

But I didn't really care

what they thought

I kept my head up high

and followed my heart

No one could stop me

from making my dreams come true

I always believed in myself

and I always will

No one can tell me

what or who I am

I am a special person

I will succeed in life

*Cipryana Smith,*
*eighth grade*

I am now in the air force
I fly a fighter jet
I still have a dream
that I've had since I was four

I wish that there would be world peace
That's why I am a jet pilot
It doesn't make any sense to me
but my heart is telling me
that I'm doing the right thing
My heart is leading me
to my dream

Next day I walk by an old bully
I say, "Hi"
"Hi," he responds. "How are you?"
I can't believe it!
It is like my first dream came true

Next day I go to the bank
I say, "Can I see how much money I have in my account?"
The teller says, "You have a million dollars"
I say, "Thanks"

I go home
My mom says she can get a better job
Same with my dad

I bet it's going to be a great life

*Vinny Simkin,*
*fourth grade*

In fifteen years I want to go around the world and
help endangered animals
I would be away from my family and friends on
trips around the world
But I'll visit them when I'm not
in another country

*Joseph DiBenedetto,*
*third grade*

If all my dreams could come true, I would be
living in the biggest castle in the world. It
would be made of a huge strawberry. In fact,
everything would be made of strawberries.

*Samantha Duarte,*
*fifth grade*

For now it's just a fantasy
a dream that will come true

A gorgeous farm with
a big barn and tons of horses

I'll ride over pastures
I'll gallop over fields
And best of all
It's a "rescue farm"

And animals will have no reason
to fear

Sunny and Pepper will gallop there
and happily rule the world

Maybe someday when I'm grown up
my rescue farm
will be real!

*Lara Briehl,*
*fifth grade*

I wish I had money
all the way up
to my neck

And I wish I had my uncle
back alive
because I miss him

We'd live in a mansion
in New York City
with animals, toys, and bicycles

I'd spend time with my uncle
My family would be very proud of me
My friends would be so happy for me

It would feel so good
to finally have
all of my dreams come true

*Jenny Russell,*
*fourth grade*

If all my dreams were to come true, I would be a veterinarian with two dogs. One of my dogs would be a Bernese Mountain Dog and the other would be a Rottweiler. Their names would be Mac and Rascal.

I probably wouldn't have a husband because I think that when you're married, it really just begins a whole lot of fighting and pain.

My house would not be too big, but not too small either. I'd live in the city, not too far from where I'd work. I'd work from 7 A.M. to 9 P.M., bringing my dogs with me to work. I would be an OK cook, but most of the time on the way home from work I'd stop somewhere and get some food.

Sure, OK, so maybe my life won't help my family become rich or get my friends a free DVD player. To tell the truth, it would hardly even make an impact on the world at all, but for those few people that I would help, I'd change their lives. Well, that's a big enough impact for me!

*Mary Clair,*
*fifth grade*

I am twenty-three years old
and the year is 2017

I look up at the first hole
at Pebble Beach

Ocean waves break
on the rocks below me

I hit the golf ball

Ahhh
Perfect shot!

I look over and see
my friends and family
as they cheer me on

I take a deep breath

There is no better feeling
than smiling and having
the rest of the world
smile back at you

*Brian McGarvey,*
*third grade*

I'm living with two dogs and an adopted daughter named Elizabeth in a blue house in the Rhode Island suburbs. Working as a writer, I have just won the Newbery Medal for a book called *Pin and Stripe* about a tiger and a wolf.

*Anna Rembar,*
*fifth grade*

My dream is to be a writer.
I will write at home, in malls,
and even at work.
I will write in airplanes and cars.
I will go to Africa
to write about the animals there.
I will go to the South Pole
to write about penguins,
whales, and seals.
I will go to the forest
to write about snakes,
beautiful rivers,
and waterfalls.

*Benjamin Vera,*
*third grade*

I stare at a blank page
Covered in nothing but lines
I cannot write

Late into the night
I begin to dream
And wonder

Drifting on a sea of ideas
I see pictures of lives
That never were

Images of imagination
After imagination
Visions from past, present, and future

Slowly, the dawn breaks
I awake from my dream
My paper is filled

*Kellum Tate,*
*fifth grade*

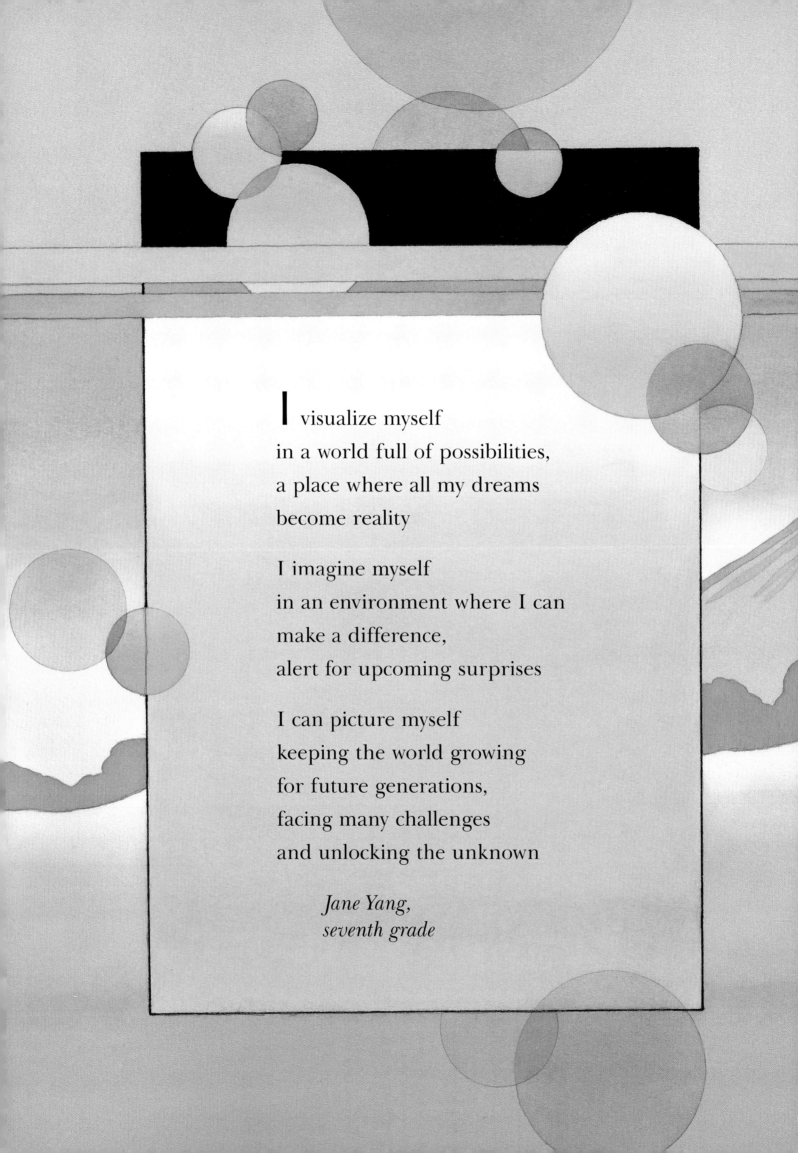

I visualize myself
in a world full of possibilities,
a place where all my dreams
become reality

I imagine myself
in an environment where I can
make a difference,
alert for upcoming surprises

I can picture myself
keeping the world growing
for future generations,
facing many challenges
and unlocking the unknown

*Jane Yang,*
*seventh grade*

Fifteen years from now
when all my dreams come true
I will be happily married
and enjoy exploring
different parts of the world

My husband and I will be
interested in caring for our environment

We'll teach our children
about the wonders of our family
and our world

I'll enjoy the blessings
of being a mom
helping my children
to create their own dreams

Fifteen years from now
wherever my journey takes me
I just want to be loved
and that is my dream for you as well

*Michelle Sims,*
*fifth grade*

I've always dreamed of being an astronaut, going on adventures, seeing planets, suns, exploring the unknown

*Aishah Jarvo,*
*fourth grade*

In ten or fifteen years I'll be king of a universe called Ry-Ry. In that universe the coolest planet of all is Deedin—*indeed* backwards. I am the poorest person there, but everything is backwards, so really I'm the richest.

There is one big problem: gravity. Yes, gravity pulls you toward the earth, but on Deedin, it pushes you away. So the most important law is never to jump.

I'm trying to invent soft stairs, because the buildings aren't upside down, but people are. So we wear helmets going up stairs.

And because everything is opposite, school takes place on the weekends, leaving the rest of the week free for fun!

*Ryan Shulman,*
*sixth grade*

I am twenty-two years old

I am a vegetarian

I am an FBI agent

I am married

I have five children

I live in the Bronx

My parents live near me

I love animals and

I want to help them

I am rich

I have a lot of houses

I have two limousines

I am very responsible

My parents will never be poor

They will not die

*Alejandro Leon,*
*third grade*

I dream of being a teacher because I like to help the little kids.

*Jasmin McFadden,*
*fifth grade*

I have a dream

No one gets teased
because of the differences
between people
There's no money in the world
No one is rich or poor
There are no more wars
Animals are not shot for sport
No one eats meat

Whenever I think I can do something . . .
I can!
I can even breathe
underwater

*Becky Plotkin,*
*fifth grade*

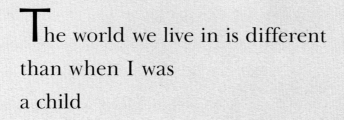

The world we live in is different
than when I was
a child

There is peace in the Middle East
and threats of terrorism
are gone

I am not afraid to
let my children
go outside

I rarely think of
the shootings and kidnappings
that took place
when I was
a child

All these things
 do not come from
  a simple dream
      but from many dreams
          from my heart
              for the future

*K.C. Butcher,*
*fifth grade*

## ACKNOWLEDGMENTS

Special thanks go to the schools that participated in the creation of *Dream Makers:*

Castle Hill Middle School, Bronx, New York
C.S. 61, Bronx, New York
Dows Lane Elementary School, Irvington, New York
E. H. Bryan School, Cresskill, New Jersey
Garden Spot Middle School, New Holland, Pennsylvania
Green Mountain Elementary School, Lakewood, Colorado
I.S. 190, New York, New York
Jeffersonville Elementary School, Jeffersonville, New York
John E. Bryan Elementary School, Morris, Alabama
Lakewood Elementary School, Congers, New York
Link Elementary School, New City, New York
The Masters School, Dobbs Ferry, New York
P.S. 8, New York, New York
P.S. 86, Bronx, New York
P.S.152, New York, New York
P.S.164, Brooklyn, New York
P.S. 306, Bronx, New York
Slater Elementary School, Lakewood, Colorado
Tamaques Elementary School, Westfield, New Jersey
West Nyack Elementary School, West Nyack, New York